Where are you going with that coal?

Where are you going with that coal?

by Roy Doty
with Leonard Maar

Doubleday & Company, Inc., Garden City, New York

This book is part of a Museum of Science and Industry/Chicago series of science books published by Doubleday & Company, Inc. The series is designed to inform, stimulate, and challenge youngsters on a wide range of scientific and technological subjects.

Library of Congress Cataloging in Publication Data

Doty, Roy, 1922–
Where are you going with that coal?

Includes index.
SUMMARY: Examines the history, the various forms, and the future uses of coal, a fossil fuel that supplies a vast amount of energy.
1. Coal—Juvenile literature. [1. Coal]
I. Maar, Leonard, joint author. II. Title.
TP32.5.D67 553'.2
ISBN 0-385-11515-6 Trade
0-385-11516-4 Prebound
Library of Congress Catalog Card Number 75–36586

Printed in the United States of America
First Edition

Contents

Preface

COAL is a black rock that burns. Like oil and natural gas, coal was once plant and animal life. That is why these are called *fossil* fuels. The energy we get from coal by burning it came from the sun and was stored in the living things. As the earth changed over the centuries, the living things were covered over by seas and dirt. When we burn coal, we are using the energy from sunlight that fell upon the earth perhaps 200 million years ago.

People have been using coal for only a few thousand years. The Greeks first described it 300 years before Christ. In China, where wood has always been in short supply, coal has been used as fuel for centuries. Coal was the fuel that provided the energy for the growth of industry in England in the 1700s.

In America, coal came into use in the early 1700s. It was the growth of the railroads in the early 1800s that created a great demand for coal and encouraged coal mining to become a large industry.

There are fifteen or more kinds of coal. Most important are anthracite, bituminous, and lignite because they are more plentiful and each has special properties. Coal has many different uses and it can be made into many products, but its main value is that it provides a source of steady, intense heat when burned. There are still trillions of tons of coal beneath the land. Some coal is found in almost every state, and America's coal deposits represent a vast source of energy. There are also rich coal deposits in many other countries of the world.

Yet, even with these great reserves of coal, we hear about an energy shortage. That, too, is an important part of the story of coal. If we can find ways to use our treasure of coal wisely, it can take us through the time of diminishing supplies of petroleum and into the future when other sources of energy can be developed.

Where are you going with that coal?

EARLY USES OF COAL. Early people found coal in seams exposed on hillsides. They used it to heat their caves and crude huts. The ancient Chinese, probably the first people to make things out of metal, may have been the first people to mine coal. The American Indians knew about coal long before the settlers came.

Because it burns with a steady, intense heat, coal replaced wood as the fuel preferred by early people as they began to use heat to separate metals from ore. Coal will not burn without oxygen, so early furnaces were built to take advantage of prevailing winds. Later, as people learned more, methods of forcing air into the furnace were developed, causing the coal fire to burn with greater heat.

Copper was probably the first metal used. It was later discovered that combinations of metals, called alloys, were harder than copper and could be sharpened and worked into different shapes. A mixture of copper and tin made bronze, for example. Iron and steel were developed as people came to know about the properties of metal and what kinds of metal were best for specific uses.

Coal gives off more heat than wood, and so it began to replace wood as the fuel for the growing metal-working industries. Also, supplies of wood were limited, huge amounts being needed to provide adequate heat. It is important that we know about fuel supply and cost, for these factors play an important part in the coal story.

STEAM ENGINES. The steam engine has been called the greatest single invention of all time. With its invention, the age of heat engines began, machines that would do the work of many men or animals. The steam engine took advantage of the fact that water, when heated, changed to a gas called steam. We think of steam as a white cloud, but it is actually invisible, the white color being droplets of water carried along with the expanding steam.

The fact that the energy in steam would do work had been known for hundreds of years before James Watt's first steam engine was developed to pump water out of the mines in England. Watt also saw how to make the steam engine work to turn machines. These early steam engines,

fueled by coal, soon made it possible for goods to be made in factories, things like cloth, clothing, tools and implements that had previously been made by hand in homes.

Plentiful coal provided the heat that spread the Industrial Revolution across Europe and, eventually, to many other countries. Then, in 1804, an Englishman, Richard Trevithick, put the steam engine on wheels in the form of a locomotive, and railroads were born.

Steam engines set the world to making things in factories, doing the work of hundreds, producing simple goods such as cloth on a mass production basis. The need for coal grew and grew, and coal mining became an important industry.

HUNDREDS of inventions followed the steam engine in quick succession. There were steam carriages, buses, tractors, steam rollers and shovels, the very important locomotive, even steam elevators, and soon, steamships. Coal continued to be in great demand, and mining intensified, hard and dangerous work employing thousands of people. In the early days, even children worked in the mines.

In America, the main source of fuel for steam engines was wood, which was plentiful. In the year 1800, only 75,000 tons of coal were mined. In the 1830s, the railroads began to stretch out across the country. The coal industry in the United States really began to grow with the railroads. It is interesting that the railroads were not only the

major users of coal, but were also the main means of moving the coal from the mine to where coal was needed.

America was slow to accept the ocean-going steamship. The steamboat, however, was in general use on rivers and the growing canal system, beginning in 1807 with Robert Fulton's famed steamboat, the *Clermont*. It was not until after the Civil War, in the late 1800s, that American coal-burning steamships began to cross the oceans.

The growing use of coal, the invention of the steam engine, the development of iron and steel, the reaching out of the railroads—these changed the world. By 1923, there were more than 9,000 operating coal mines in the United States employing more than 700,000 people.

COAL GAS. When coal burns, it releases gases. As coal was more widely used, it became clear that these gases had value. In the late 1700s, coal gas was used to light English homes. Whale oil, which had been used for lighting, was harder to get and had become too expensive. Coal gas was the most readily available alternative. It was used in England well into the 1900s, and in parts of the United States into the mid-1960s.

America's whaling industry was able to supply whale oil at a reasonable price into the early 1800s, but by 1840, it had become too expensive and Americans had begun using coal gas for lighting. In 1859 there were sixty refineries making "illuminating gas" from coal. Heating,

lighting, and cooking were done with this abundant manufactured gas. Coal gas had become an important source of energy.

With the invention in the late 1800s of means to provide electricity to homes, electric lighting became the most popular illumination. The manufacture of coal gas for home use sharply declined, ending almost completely in the 1960s. Moreover, petroleum had been discovered in 1859, and America began to shift from coal to oil for home heating. The coal industry began to decline from its peak just after World War I, although it continued to play an important part in countries where supplies of electricity and petroleum remained scarce and expensive.

ELECTRIC GENERATION. With coal as the source of energy, and with iron and steel boilers to contain the high-pressure steam, tremendous power had been harnessed. Watt's first engine led the way to the development of steam generation of electricity.

While the steam engine was being perfected, a great deal was being learned about electricity. Benjamin Franklin, Michael Faraday, and many others provided the knowledge that made it possible for Thomas Edison to design the first coal-fired, steam-generating electric power plants. Three of them went into operation in 1882, two in England and one in New York City, the latter known as the Pearl Street Station. It served fifty-nine customers.

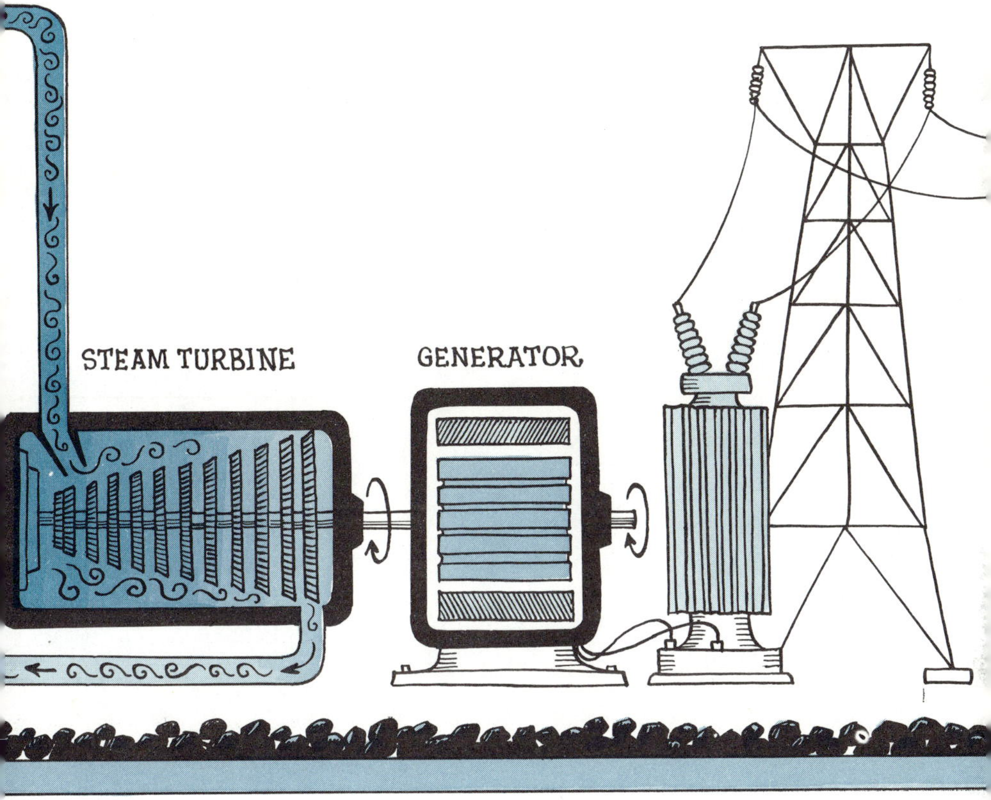

There are several different kinds of steam electric plants. The basic elements are shown above. The heat boils the water, turning it to steam. The steam forces the turbine to spin, and a central shaft turns the generator, which changes the energy into electricity. If you look carefully, you will see, at the right end of the moving grate, smoke rising up the stack and ash falling into the ash pit. Smoke and ash are two factors that cause pollution.

Cleaning the smoke is a big problem, one that many companies are spending a lot of time and money to solve. Air pollution is one of the major objections to using coal as fuel, and many power plants use oil instead, although it, too, can cause air pollution.

THE ELECTRICITY that comes from the power plants is a clean, versatile source of energy. Electricity has changed our world. Can you imagine your home or your school without electricity? Think of how it must have been for the people who lived before electricity was available.

In the school above, see how many things are run by electricity. Make a list of them and then see if you can find more in your school. Some rainy day when you are looking for something to do, make the same kind of list for your home.

Wherever we go, we see the wires that bring electricity from the power plant to our homes, schools, stores, and office buildings. Electricity powers all kinds of factory

motors and lights our streets and traffic lights. Special lines connect our telephones so that we can call anywhere, any time.

We take electric power for granted, for it is a part of our lives. We don't think about electricity when we flick a switch—we want light, music from the radio, a picture on the television. But it is the energy from the coal, changed into electricity, that makes all this possible.

And what we use in our homes and schools is just a small amount compared to what it takes to run the giant, powerful rollers that press out sheets of steel, or the precisely controlled rollers that squeeze wood fibers into thin sheets of paper.

AS ELECTRIC POWER became readily available, it was put to work in many ways. The first streetcar, or trolley, took its first trip in 1874. It clattered past electric signs, past factories with electric machinery. In Boston in 1897, the first subway opened. The second such underground rail system was New York City's, in 1904.

Slowly, electricity spread across the country, out to the smallest towns and to the farm land. Coal was the fuel, and millions of tons were mined to meet the growing demand for power. The first thirty years of this century were the golden time for the black rock that burns.

But then, as petroleum became more plentiful and less expensive, cars and buses began to replace the trolleys and

commuter trains. Big trucks powered by diesel fuel began to carry more and more freight. Even the railroads, coal's partner in growth, changed over to oil. Slowly, the coal furnace gave way to the oil burner in American homes.

Coal consumption fell off dramatically. Coal was much harder to transport than oil. Natural gas was coming into use as a fuel. As progress continued, we learned how to use coal much more efficiently. In other words, we learned how to get more work out of each ton of coal. In 1919, it took more than a ton and a half of coal to make a ton of steel. Today, it takes a little over a half ton. The same thing was happening in the production of electricity. Three quarters of a ton of coal now does the work of three tons.

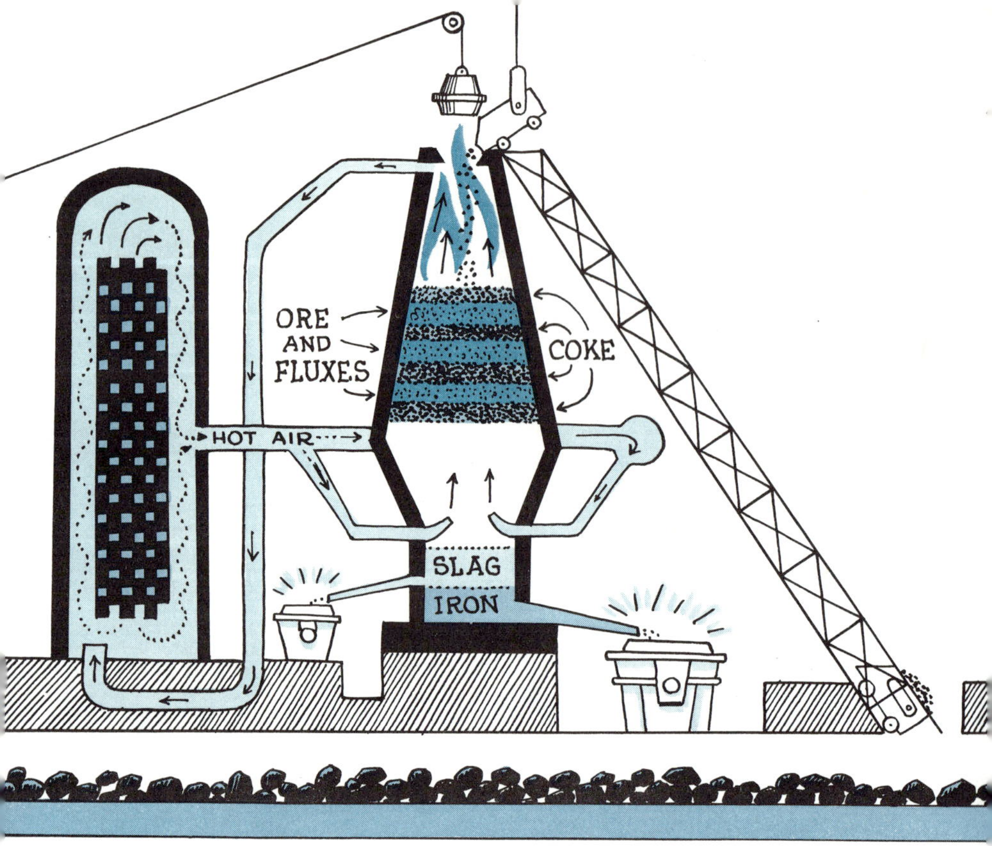

IRON AND STEEL. Producing electricity is still coal's Number 1 job, but second is the making of iron and steel. Coal is used in two ways in the metal industry, as direct fuel to provide heat, and as "coke." Coal is changed into coke by burning in special ovens that exclude most of the air and allow the impurities to be carried away for other uses. Coke is used both as fuel for the blast furnaces and as a reducing agent inside the furnace to separate the iron from the ore. This is a heat and chemical process.

The liquid iron taken from the furnace is usually used directly in making steel. Steel is an alloy, a mixture of metals. Different kinds of steel for different uses are made

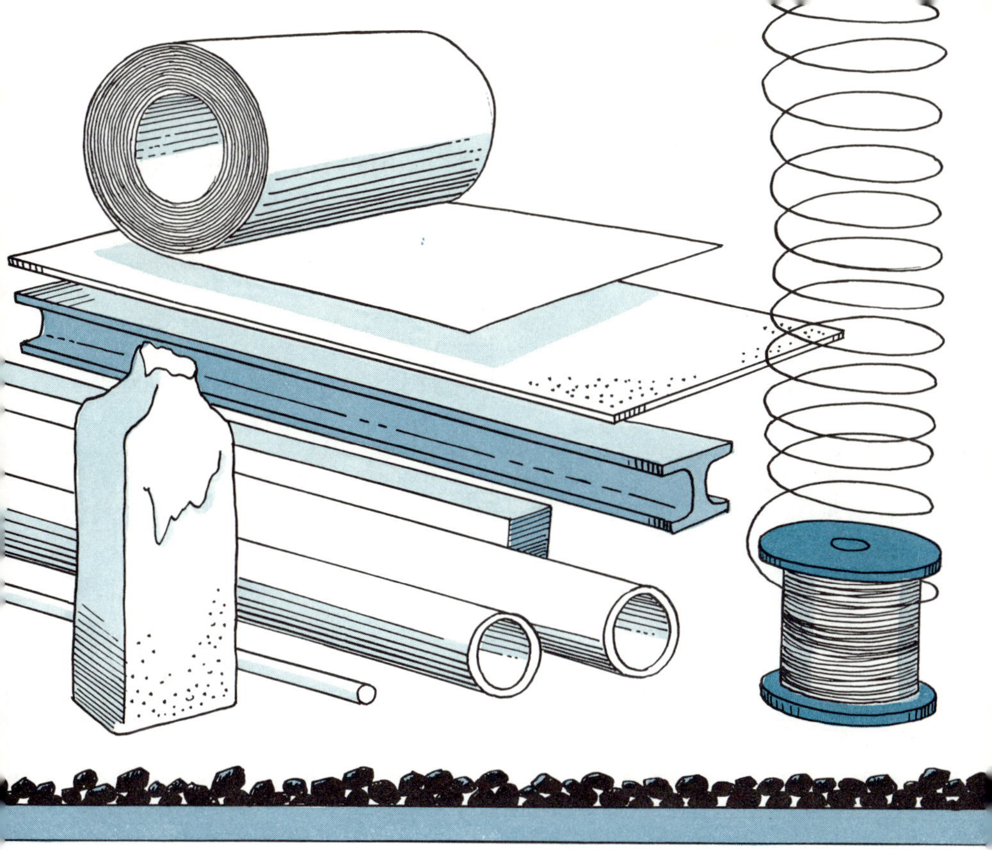

by adding various metals and carbon to the liquid iron.

First used in England, coke is coal that has been baked to remove its impurities. It is similar to charcoal, made from wood, which was the primary fuel in making iron in America, both because it was plentiful and because it was thought to make a better product. For many years, the gases and other by-products produced in making iron and steel were wasted. Today we can find a use for almost every form of the energy released by coal.

Skyscrapers, cars, ships, pots, and pans. Iron and steel are really important to modern life. And the energy from coal makes it all possible.

COAL BY-PRODUCTS. The study of blast-furnace gases, and knowledge gained in making coke and town gas, led to the making of other by-products from coal gas.

The gases from the coal being carbonized to make coke pass out of the coke ovens and up through pipes into a collecting tank, where they are cooled. As the gas cools, coal tar and ammonia liquor form. The remaining gas is treated with absorbing oil, which removes what is called light oil. The light oil is refined by distillation, which simply means that it is broken down into usable chemicals.

Coal tar can be used directly as a fuel. It can be distilled—broken up into parts. These parts are used in making roofing material, road surfacing, special coatings, and

certain kinds of pipe. Creosote, a valuable wood preservative, is made. Coal tar chemicals are used in making dyes and pigments to color paints, varnishes, lacquers, wallpapers, and plastics.

Plasticizers are produced which are added to plastics to make them softer and more flexible. Other parts are used as gasoline additives, hydraulic fluid, resins, varnishes and adhesives, fabric waterproofing, and solvents. There are flavorings and perfumes which include synthetic oil of wintergreen, vanillin, menthol, and citronella. We know these as flavors or odors in foods and drugs, as scents in soap, cosmetics, and other products.

THE AMMONIA LIQUOR is changed into ammonia sulphate and was once a very valuable product used as a fertilizer. Better methods of making ammonia have been developed and so have reduced the value of this coal by-product. But some is still used in fertilizers and as a neutralizing agent.

Far more valuable are the light oils stripped from the coal gas. Hundreds of chemical compounds are obtainable by distillation, but the major ones are benzol, toluol, xylols, and naphthas.

Benzene is used in making plastic, phenols, synthetic fibers, detergents, aniline used in making dye, solvents,

DDT and other insecticides. It is also used in adhesives, detergents, explosives, fungicide, and synthetic rubber.

Toluol is used to make the powerful explosive TNT. It is also used to make many chemicals, such as benzaldehyde, benzoic acid, artificial musk, saccharin, and a number of dyes. It finds extensive use as a solvent.

There are three xylols present. In purified form, they are used as raw materials in making a variety of chemicals, mothproofing agents, drugs, and dyes, and as a solvent for such things as airplane dopes, lacquers and varnishes, paints and enamels, and rubber cement. The naphthas are used primarily as solvents, making various surface coatings, and in floor tiles.

THE STUDY of how these components of coal can be identified and separated is part of the field of organic chemistry. This branch of chemistry is concerned with the substances that make up living matter, which all contain the element carbon. Since most organic compounds also contain hydrogen, it is called the chemistry of hydrocarbons.

Of the parts of the remaining coal gas, methane is an interesting one to look at. Compounds of carbon and hydrogen are made up of molecules of different arrangements of atoms of each of these two elements. Methane is the simplest, containing four hydrogen atoms arranged around a central carbon atom. This is expressed chemically as CH_4. All of the other compounds from coal gas

are made up of various numbers of carbon and hydrogen atoms. Methane is used in plastics, anesthetics, synthetic rubber, alcohols, liquid fuels, protective coatings, refrigerants, and solvents. Methane is the main component of natural gas, so we can see how natural gas, coal, and petroleum are directly related.

Ethane is used in resins, synthetic fibers, drugs, and insecticides. Ethylene is used in antifreeze, anesthetics, plastics, and solvents.

Of all the coal by-products, coke is by far the most important. The coal chemicals have largely been replaced by the same chemicals extracted from petroleum, although they are still important in some uses.

COAL AND COKE AS FUEL. While petroleum and natural gas have replaced coal because they have been cheaper and more easily available, coal is still the chief fuel in many places. Generating electricity is the largest single use. The making of iron and steel is second.

Wherever intense heat is required, coal can be used as the fuel. In the making of ceramics, such as bathtubs, washbasins, and sinks, heat for kilns, or drying ovens, comes from burning coal. The same is true in making cement, in the papermaking industry, and in some chemical manufacturing. Coal is the fuel in smelting various metals and in metal-working processes. Coal is even used to make

steam in the atomic fuel enrichment plants. Thousands of factories are heated by coal, which also produces the steam needed in many industrial processes.

There are still some homes in the United States where coal is used for heat. Many big buildings, such as schools, hospitals, hotels, and apartment buildings, rely on coal.

During the early 1970s, as we began to realize that petroleum and natural gas were in short supply and would eventually be used up, many manufacturers returned to using coal. If the prices of other sources of energy continue to rise, coal, which is plentiful, will be used more and more.

COAL GASIFICATION DURING WORLD WAR II. Each of the three fossil fuels—coal, petroleum, and natural gas—can be converted into the other two by changing their content of carbon and hydrogen. Thus, coal can be made into gasoline, diesel oil, and kerosene.

The two original processes for converting coal to liquid fuel were both invented in Germany. The Bergius process was developed just after World War I. It was used commercially in Germany, Japan, and England—countries poor in liquid fuels. The second process was invented by two Germans, Franz Fischer and Hans Tropsch. There have been variations of these two methods, but they are the best known.

During the early 1970s, as we began to realize that petro-motor fuels of all kinds. Through the development of a crash program, coal was converted to the liquid fuels needed to run the German war machine, as much as 12,000 barrels a day. It takes about five tons of coal to make one ton of liquid fuel.

The fact that coal conversion to liquid fuels was done in wartime Germany shows how inventive man can be when necessity demands it. Several important mining techniques were also developed in Germany during the war because of the huge demand for coal to make iron and steel, to make the machines of war, and to make the fuel for them.

SOUTH AFRICA'S SYNTHETIC PETROLEUM. The Republic of South Africa, because that country wishes to be independent of the oil-exporting nations, and because she is short of petroleum, operates the world's largest coal-conversion facility. The country has both a plentiful supply of coal and cheap labor, two factors that encouraged the development of this unique project.

The SASOL (South African Coal, Oil, and Gas Company, Ltd.) complex is located near a vast coal field. The process used to convert the coal to liquid fuel is the Fischer-Tropsch method, much the same process used in Germany.

Here is how it works. First, the coal is burned with oxygen and steam at very high temperatures so that it re-

leases great amounts of gas. This gas is cleaned, purified of unwanted components. It is then re-formed to obtain the right carbon/hydrogen balance. Next, it goes to synthesis plants, or refineries, where it is broken up into its various fractions. Some crude oil and naphtha are additives to the process.

Just as with natural gas or petroleum, the refining process produces several basic families of chemicals.

The primary objective of the SASOL project was to obtain liquid fuels—gasoline, diesel oil, and kerosene—and chemicals to make synthetic rubber. In the process, methane gas is also obtained and is used as pipeline gas for cooking, heating, and some industrial applications.

PETROCHEMICALS are produced at SASOL. These are rearranged compounds of carbon and hydrogen so as to produce the products desired. Coal also fuels an electric generating plant that serves the thirty plants in the complex.

As you can see from the illustrations, a tremendous variety of coal by-products are made, including plastics, fibers, films, and chemicals that go into paints, detergents, cosmetics, antifreeze, anesthetics, and so on.

Plastics are rapidly becoming the world's most widely used material. They have many advantages: They are light in weight, colorful, and easy to form, cost little to produce, are easy to keep clean, and some can even be

sterilized. Plastics can be very strong, they won't rust, and they resist many chemicals. It is easy to see why plastics are highly useful, and why they are an important product from the coal-conversion process.

Other important chemicals produced go into building materials, road surfacing, drugs and medicines, fertilizers and pesticides, food additives, detergents and cleansers, synthetic rubber additives, solvents and paints. As the chemists and engineers working at the SASOL project see it, they will eventually be able to produce all of the same by-products from coal that other countries make from petroleum.

COAL—TRANSPORTATION FUEL OF THE FUTURE. Sooner or later we are going to find petroleum in short supply. There are many guesses as to how long the world's supply will last, but the thing to remember is that there is only just so much buried underground. And as petroleum becomes ever scarcer, it will cost more.

It is now estimated that the United States has enough minable coal to last for several hundred years. It is possible that someday we will rely on coal for our liquid fuels. Research is well under way to find methods to convert coal into affordable liquid fuels.

The South African SASOL project and the early German processes have shown that converting coal to gasoline

and other fuels is possible, however expensive. Another interesting approach is being tested and that is to convert coal to methanol, known commonly as wood alcohol. It is currently the only liquid fuel that we know how to make from coal at a price we would be willing to pay.

Methanol is already used in racing-car engines. It will burn readily in automobile engines, and it burns cleaner than gasoline. It produces only half the energy per gallon that gasoline does, however.

One thing is sure. The United States has one fifth of the world's coal reserves. The world's supply of petroleum and natural gas is shrinking. Sooner or later, coal will be our major fuel source once again.

COAL CONVERSION TO GAS. We must remember that when we talk about gas, we are referring to a non-liquid. In many of our homes, natural gas from wells drilled into the ground provides us with a relatively inexpensive fuel. Natural gas is used in cooking, in home heating, and for appliances such as clothes driers. It is brought to the home through pipelines, sometimes over distances of thousands of miles.

Much like petroleum, natural gas is found in underground reservoirs. There is only just so much of it, and in the years ahead, we will find this type of fuel in short supply.

There are a number of methods being developed to find

a way to make a synthetic natural gas from coal. We know that it can be done, and finding the best, most economical way is the purpose of current research. Natural gas is an important fuel in factories and as raw material for the petrochemical industry. It provides the energy in many glass factories, in making cement and paper, and in metal making and forming operations.

If we develop solar-energy home heating to the fullest extent, we will have homes heated by the sun, needing only backup heating systems. Coal gas could supply the needed fuel. This combination of alternatives to using petroleum-based home heating oil and natural gas can help to make us much less dependent on oil.

THE COAL-OIL-GAS REFINERY. It seems logical that a plant that would produce all of the liquid fuels and the chemical by-products from coal in one operation would be the best answer to the problem of replacing petroleum. Coal would feed in one end of the plant, and gasoline, pipeline gas, diesel oil, liquid petroleum gas (bottled gas), sulphur, and other chemicals would come out the other.

This isn't just a dream. Such a refinery process has already been studied, and the necessary technology has been developed. The major problem, as in many of the coal-conversion projects, is that of cost.

Such a refinery would require 57,000 tons of coal and 7,740 tons of oxygen each day. It would produce about

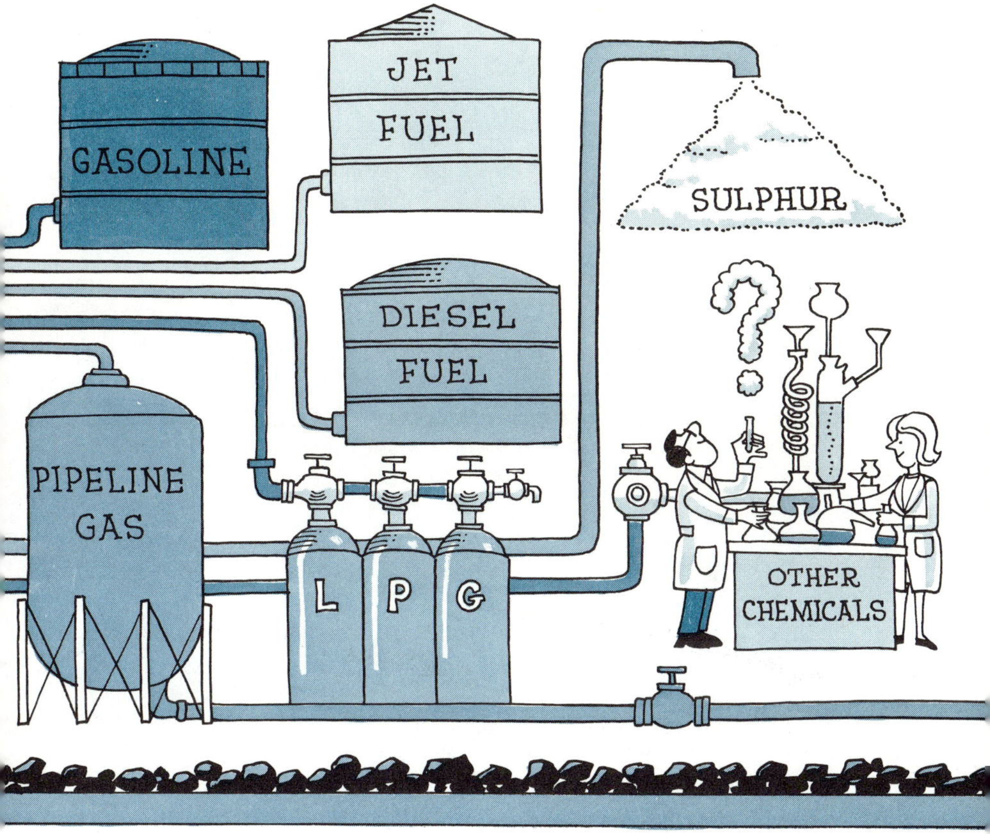

1,800 tons of sulphur, 7,660 tons of pipeline gas, 1,980 tons of liquid petroleum gas, and 14,660 tons of refinery oil from which gasoline and other fuels would be made.

In considering coal-conversion processes, we must be concerned with the recovery of the energy coal could produce if it were simply burned as fuel. In the coal-oil-gas refinery, only about a quarter of the energy potential of the coal is lost. So the plant is 75 per cent efficient.

The cost must be measured against the amount of money required to find and produce petroleum and natural gas. As our reserves of these other fuels are used up, and the cost of imported oil and gas rises, coal conversion becomes a much more attractive undertaking.

FUTURE PROCESSES. In addition to converting coal to gas or liquid fuel, research is going on to find ways to remove the sulphur and other impurities from coal.

A study is being made for a plant to have clean coal as its major end product. It would use plentiful high-sulphur coal and produce a clean solid fuel which, when burned, would create little or no air pollution.

Still another concept is called the fluidized bed boiler. It can burn high-sulphur coal to produce steam, concentrating the sulphur in a gas so that it can be recovered and not released into the air. As coal becomes more widely used to replace petroleum, many other ways to use it will be developed.

Will we run out of coal?

COAL is our most abundant natural fuel resource. With our huge reserves, it will be hundreds of years before they are used up. But using up our fuel resources is really not the problem—it is how wisely we use them.

Although coal is our most plentiful fossil fuel, we use it to meet only 20 per cent of our fuel needs. Oil and gas reserves are much smaller, yet we use them to fill 80 per cent of our energy needs. In other words, we are using the fuels in shortest supply to meet the greatest share of our energy requirements.

THERE ARE about 3,600 billion tons of coal in the earth's crust in the United States. We can recover between 5 and 8 per cent of that, a supply that will last for more than three hundred years. We can probably get as much as 20 to 30 per cent if we are willing to dig deeper, mine small deposits, and develop new mining techniques.

Coal mining is a business. The mineowners extract the coal so that they can sell it. They must own or lease the land, buy the mining equipment, hire the mine workers. They are also responsible for the safe operation of the mines. And there are dangers such as cave-ins and poisonous gas. There is also the danger to the men who work in the mines of a lung ailment caused by the coal dust.

Some coal deposits are near the surface of the earth. Some are deep. Some coal seams are thick and yield large quantities of coal, some are thin and not worth working. We must remember, too, that some kinds of coal are in more demand than others. Where coal appears near the

surface, a type of surface mining is done. This often tears up large areas of land making it unattractive and worthless for farming or recreation.

Taking all this, and government regulations, coal mining can be a risky investment. Yet the coal industry hopes to increase the production of coal from about 700 million tons in 1977 to 1.3 billion tons in 1980 and 2.1 billion tons by 1985. Where will it come from?

The coal deposits in the western states of Montana, North Dakota, Wyoming, Colorado, Utah, Arizona, and New Mexico make up 72 per cent of our reserves. Much of this coal is low in sulphur content, and almost half of it is close to the surface.

Surface mining is done as follows. First, the topsoil is removed and stockpiled so that it can later be put back in place. Then the hard second layer of dirt is drilled, blasted loose, and removed. The uncovered coal is drilled, blasted loose, and trucked to the railroad line. The damage to the land can be considerable.

Despite all of the problems, it looks as though large amounts of coal can be mined in the western states to meet the growing demand.

MINING COAL, as difficult a task as it is, only starts the long chain that provides the energy for making electricity or iron and steel. The coal has to be taken to the power plant or the steel mill.

Coal is bulky, chunks of black rock. A large generating station burns as much as 5,000 tons of coal a day. It would take an entire trainload of coal to meet that demand. In fact, unit trains, which may have a hundred or more railroad cars, can carry from 4,000 to 10,000 tons in a load. These trains run from the mine to the user. The railroads carry almost three fourths of the coal mined in the United States.

In many areas of our country there are great systems of rivers and canals called inland waterways. Coal is moved along these waterways by barges towed by powerful little boats. About 12 per cent of the nation's coal is transported in this manner.

A fairly new development involves mixing coal with water and pumping it through what is called a slurry pipeline. Two such pipelines have been built, and one is still in use—the 273-mile-long Black Mesa line running from a mine in Arizona to a power plant in Nevada. It moves 4.8 million tons of coal a year and was built over land too rough for a railroad. There are six new coal-water slurry pipelines now on the drawing boards, one of which will run for over a thousand miles from Gillette, Wyoming, to

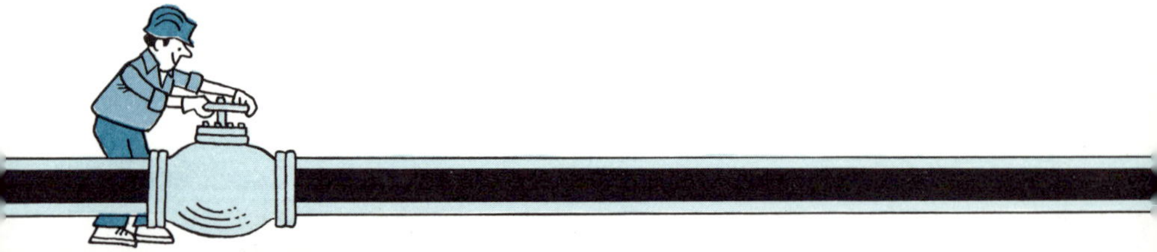

White Bluff, Arkansas. There is much argument about how these pipelines will affect the railroads' business. The pipelines will need special help from the federal government if they are to succeed.

Of course, the most efficient way to use coal is to have the power plant right at the mine. This is called "coal by wire." High-voltage transmission wires carry the electricity to customers many miles away. For example, electricity generated at mines in New Mexico, Arizona, and Wyoming is now being sent as far away as California.

Moving coal to the customer is a vast job. But at the mine, coal has to be moved from the place where it is dug, out of the mine. Many kinds of transportation are used in the mines. Great conveyor belts move the coal in some mines, while in others, tractor-trailers are used. Shuttle carts are common in some mines, hauling coal from the mine face to dumps outside. Some pipelines are used with the coal-water mixture pumping continuous streams of mined coal out of the mine. Even pneumatic pipelines are being considered with air as the carrying medium.

Moving coal is a most important part of the story of the black rock that burns. Millions upon millions of tons have to be moved each year, from mine face to storage, from storage to the user. Just as new mining methods and new coal-conversion methods will have to be developed to meet the increased demand for coal, new, cheaper transportation systems will also have to be devised.

AMERICANS represent only about 6 per cent of the world's population. We consume almost 33 per cent of the world's commercial energy.

Obviously, we will have to mine more coal, and find and produce more oil and natural gas. Because our coal reserves far surpass our reserves of oil and gas, we must turn to coal as the source of energy to carry us through until new sources of energy can be developed.

But people have other needs besides energy. If we want to surface-mine coal, then we must be willing to pay the cost of restoring the land so that it can be used for ranching and recreation. If we want to dig deeper mines, we must make them safer for the men who work in them. If we burn more coal, we must find ways to avoid air pollution. Our need to preserve and protect our environment must be a prime consideration in our search for energy.

Interestingly enough, all of these considerations are a part of both our government's concern and that of private industry as we cope with energy problems. Coal companies are working to reclaim the land after surface mining. Industry and governmental agencies are working to cope with the problems of air and water pollution.

Coal is one of our most valuable national treasures. The black rock that burns will play a necessary part in our lives for many years still to come.

Glossary

ALLOY: the mixture of two or more metals, sometimes with other substances, to make a new metal, such as steel.

AMMONIA: a chemical by-product of hydrocarbons. Ammonia's nitrogen content makes it valuable in making fertilizers.

BY-PRODUCT: any substance produced in the hydrocarbon refining process.

CARBON: a nonmetallic element, found in all living matter.

COAL: one of the fossil fuels, a hydrocarbon formed from living matter by pressure, heat, and chemical action beneath the changing crust of the earth. The black rock that burns.

COAL CONVERSION: the process of changing coal into liquid fuels such as gasoline, diesel oil, and fuel oil.

COAL GASIFICATION: the process of changing coal into coal gases which can then be refined into by-products.

COAL TAR: an important, sticky, oily by-product formed during the coal-conversion or gasification processes.

COKE: an important fuel made by heating coal in the absence of air to remove the impurities.

CREOSOTE: an oily by-product of coal used as a wood preservative.

CRUDE OIL: unrefined petroleum as it comes from the well.

ELEMENTS: simple substances, such as carbon, hydrogen, oxygen, and nitrogen, that cannot be reduced to simpler forms.

ENERGY: the capacity to do work. Coal is a raw material used to produce *power*.

FOSSIL FUELS: those substances—coal, natural gas, petroleum—formed by pressure, heat, and chemical action, as living matter was buried by the earth's changing crust.

HYDROCARBONS: substances containing the elements hydrogen and carbon.

HYDROGEN: the lightest of all known elements. An element almost always found in organic matter.

INDUSTRIAL REVOLUTION: the period of time from 1750 to 1830 when coal became the fuel for steam engines used in manufacturing. The changing time when goods were made by machine instead of by hand.

LIGHT OIL: a useful by-product of the hydrocarbon refining process.

LIQUID PETROLEUM GAS: gases from wells, or produced in the refinery process held in a liquid form under pressure. Commonly known as bottled gas.

METHANE, ETHANE, ETHYLENE: useful by-products of the hydrocarbon refining process. Basic materials which can be broken down into useful products.

METHANOL: an alcohol that is a hydrocarbon by-product that can be used as a fuel.

NAPHTHA: a hydrocarbon by-product used in cleaning fluids and in many chemical and industrial processes.

NATURAL GAS: a gas found beneath the earth's crust, obtained by drilling wells, in the same manner as oil wells.

ORGANIC CHEMISTRY: the study of the chemistry of organic, or living, matter.

OXYGEN: an element that forms about one fifth of the air. Animals and plants cannot live without oxygen, nor can fire burn without it.

PLASTICS: materials such as nylon and styrene made from hydrocarbon chemicals.

POLLUTION: making something dirty, as the sulphur gases from some kinds of coal make the air unfit to breathe.

POWER: energy that has been changed into a form that can do useful work. Coal is burned to heat water to make steam that spins the turbines to make electricity, producing electric power.

REFINING: the process of breaking down a raw substance, such as coal or petroleum, into its usable parts. The freeing of such substances of impurities.

SULPHUR: a yellow nonmetallic element often found in hydrocarbons. Sulphur changes into a dirty gas when burned.

SURFACE MINING: the mining of coal, or other ores, found near the surface of the earth.

SYNTHETICS: substances or materials made of elements combined to duplicate a natural product, such as nylon thread made from hydrocarbons to imitate silk, or liquid fuels produced from the solid coal.

Index

ROY DOTY is a nationally known free-lance artist whose work regularly appears in numerous major publications such as *Newsweek, Business Week,* and *The New York Times.* He is familiar to *Popular Science* readers as author-cartoonist of the monthly "Wordless Workshop," and his "Laugh-In" newspaper comic strip was nationally syndicated. An inventor and do-it-yourself hobbyist, Mr. Doty is the creator of the Popular Science Picture Clock Kit. He lives in Connecticut with his authoress wife and four children in one of the world's few solar-heated homes, which he helped design himself.

LEONARD MAAR is a professional writer who works in corporate communication and advertising. He has written for numerous national magazines and, with his wife, is the author of a cookbook. The Maars live on the Connecticut shore with their two children, three cats, and two dogs.

Where are you going with
that coal?